Wedding Papercrafts

Wedding Papercrafts

35 BEAUTIFUL
EASY-TO-MAKE PROJECTS FOR
THAT SPECIAL OCCASION

Ann Brownfield & Jane Cassini

CICO BOOKS

LONDON NEW YORK

Published in 2009 by CICO Books
An imprint of
Ryland Peters & Small
20–21 Jockey's Fields   519 Broadway, 5th Floor
London WC1R 4BW   New York, NY 10012

www.cicobooks.com

10 9 8 7 6 5 4 3 2 1

A CIP catalog record for this book is available from
the Library of Congress and the British Library.

ISBN-13: 978 1 906094 76 8

Printed in China

Editor: Robin Gurdon
Designer: Janet James
Stylists: Ann Brownfield and Jane Cassini
Photographer: Caroline Arber

Contents

Introduction

Your wedding is a very special celebration, and one where every detail should reflect your individual spirit. Within these pages you'll find ways to beautifully present the ideas that will personalize your wedding, adding the vital finishing touches that can make such a difference. While some papercrafts are simple and others more complex, all act as a springboard for your own creativity and choices.

You'll discover inspirational ways of using different types of papers—creating delicate interplay between opacity and translucency, mixing the old and faded with the crisp and pristine, and combining gorgeous colors and textures—and see how the addition of a sparkling button, lustrous pearl, length of slender ribbon, or gilded thread can embellish and enhance.

From the exciting preparations through the blissful day to the final thank-you letters and keepsakes, these romantic projects will inspire your imagination and impart paper designs with an unexpected, fresh and elegant twist. Whether you are planning the simplest of ceremonies or the most lavish affair, the beauty and versatility of paper shines through and will help create your perfect wedding.

Ann & Jane

1

Preparing for the Day

This special time before the actual day is the period where your attention to detail will be sure to delight everyone. Wedding invitations don't have to be formal, just truly romantic, whilst defining your own unique style. Try mixing faded antique and vintage ephemera with crisp glassine and watercolor papers to create these lovely wedding cards and envelopes—sweetly old-fashioned but with an essential contemporary edge.

Ephemera Wedding Invitations

Enchantingly romantic wedding invitations are created from ephemera salvaged from Victorian and Edwardian cards. Delicate filigree edgings, embossed borders, entwined initials, and exquisite watercolor cameos take on an air of sophistication when placed on a luxurious ivory paper. Pretty vintage 'finds'—a heart-shaped locket or a miniature fan—are perfect to enhance each invitation and reflect the spirit of the forthcoming day.

Materials

300gsm hot-pressed watercolor
  paper
Fine utility paper or tissue paper
Cutting board
Craft knife
Metal safety ruler
Pencil
Bone folder
Ephemera papers
Vintage gold thread
Lockets and hearts
Scissors
Double-sided tape
Multi-purpose adhesive
Spray adhesive
Pen and black ink
Eraser

Optional (to deckle paper)
Water jar
Paint brush

1 With ruler, pencil, cutting board, and craft knife, measure out and cut the watercolor paper to 7⅝ x 10in (19.5 x 25cm). Use the bone folder to fold the paper in half, making a card 7⅝ x 5in (19.5 x 12.5cm), with the wrong side of the paper on the inside. If possible keep any deckle edging to the front of the invitation card, for decorative effect. Alternatively, create your own deckle edge: dampen the paper edges with a paint brush dipped in water and carefully tear the damp paper against the edge of the ruler.

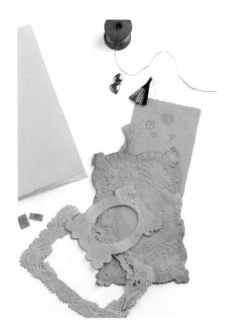

2 Assemble a selection of ephemera papers, such as vintage greeting cards, old postcards, and cameos. Keep to prettily colored papers that have a pleasing texture. Find vintage gold thread and a selection of gold lockets and hearts, one for each card. Vintage jewellery and ephemera can be easily found in flea markets and antique fairs. Also look out for old lettering from cards and postcards, which can be cut out and re-used.

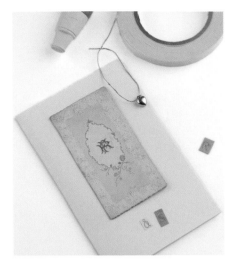  

3 Arrange a selection on the front cover of each invitation card, using a mixture of images, a gold charm, and a few cut-out letters forming the initials of the bride and groom. Use double-sided tape or adhesive to fix these to the cover. Thread a charm with the gold thread and loop it on to the card, then glue in place.

4 With ruler, pencil, cutting board, and craft knife, measure out a rectangle 7½ x 4¾in (19 x 12cm) from the watercolor paper. This will be for the written invitation. Work out the position and wording of the invitation with pencil and ruler first. This can be rubbed out when you have finished. Using pen and ink write each card, then glue into the inside back cover of the invitation card, using spray adhesive.

5 To fashion the lining use pencil and ruler, craft knife and cutting board to cut the fine utility paper or tissue paper to 7⅜ x 10in (19.5 x 25cm). Fold in half to 7⅜ x 5in (19.5 x 12.5cm), with the wrong side of the paper on the inside, and slip into the center of the invitation card. Tie gold thread around the spine, to hold the paper lining in place. Tie with a knot or pretty bow.

HINT

Capture the pleasure of collecting intriguing paper ephemera—postcards, greetings, and 'calling' cards—for the delicate and tantalizing qualities of the papers, typefaces, and images used during these eras. This ephemera can be re-used enabling its distinctive character to be revealed in a fresh, contemporary way. Don't worry if a card is damaged; even a fragment or layer of filigree paper can be gently peeled away from its base—hold it in the steam of a kettle first to soften any glue. Remember, imperfections are part of their unique charm, but if a stubborn mark really bothers you just remove with a good quality 'putty' eraser.

Wedding Invitation Envelope with Seal

An elegant envelope cut from the same paper used for the invitations and featuring an elongated 'V' design is sealed with a delightful emblem—a vintage illustration edged with gold. Either create each seal individually or photocopy your chosen image and repeat to create multiples. A final touch of a locket suspended on old-gold thread completes the picture.

Materials

300gsm hot-pressed
  watercolor paper
Ephemera papers
Gold paper doily
Vintage gold thread
Gold lockets and hearts
Cutting board
Craft knife
Metal safety ruler
Pencil
Bone folder
Scissors
Double-sided tape

1 Using the template on page 128 as a guide, cut out an envelope from the watercolor paper, using the ruler, pencil, cutting board, and craft knife. The envelope should measure 25in (63cm) long. Working with the wrong side of the paper facing you and using the bone folder, crease along the fold marks indicated on the template. Fold toward you. Then turn the two side flaps firmly inward. Attach double-sided tape to the side flaps, on the right side of the paper. Fold the bottom flap upward to form the envelope and attach to the side flaps, with the flaps on the inside. Press firmly together.

2 For each seal cut out a rectangle from the watercolor paper 2 x 3⅛in (5 x 8cm). Trim this with the gold doily paper by cutting a fine strip off the scalloped edge and glue this to the back of the seal using double-sided tape, so that only about ⅛in (2mm) of the gold scallop shows. To decorate the seal choose an image from your selection of ephemera papers or simply photocopy one image in multiples. Wind gold thread around the seal, attach a gold locket or heart and fix at the back. Use this seal to fasten the flap of the envelope, with a double-sided tape backing.

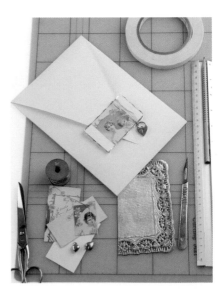

Wedding Party Invitations

An eclectic mix of old and new papers, heart-shaped trinkets, and charms, along with a handwritten card placed into a paper pocket, will create these appealing invitations. Lined with glassine pages, looped with ribbons, and with vintage gold thread linking the charms together, each one differs and is sure to be treasured by the recipient.

Materials

90 or 150gsm white
  watercolor paper
300gsm cream card
40gsm textured glassine paper
Gold tissue paper
Vintage brown paper
Thin ribbon
Pearls
Gold or silver hearts
Vintage gold thread
Cutting board
Craft knife
Metal safety ruler
Pencil
Scissors
Spray adhesive
Double-sided tape
Thick embroidery needle
Black rollerball pen
Nib pen and gold ink

1 Using the ruler, pencil, cutting board, and craft knife, cut out rectangles of the white watercolor paper 3⅛ x 14in (8 x 36cm). Fold in half to make a card 3⅛ x 7in (8 x 18cm). Cut two rectangles of the cream card and two rectangles of the glassine to 4 x 7½in (10 x 19cm). Cut a rectangle 2 x 6in (5 x 15cm) for the front pocket, from brown vintage paper. The paper used for these invitations was the inside wrapper from an old roll of vintage ribbon. Alternatively use ordinary brown wrapping paper and crimp the edges with pinking shears to get a pretty, decorative effect.

2 To assemble the invitation card, spray the inside of the white folded watercolor paper with adhesive spray. Position both cream cards inside the white watercolor paper, so that they butt up to the spine, with ⅜in (1cm) of card showing at top, right and bottom edges. Press to glue the cream cards in place. Using a thin strip of double-sided tape, glue one sheet of glassine paper to the inside of the front cream card, and one sheet inside the back card, just at the spine edge. Write the name of the bride and groom on the front of the brown paper, fold in at each end, and glue with double-sided tape to form the pocket. Decorate with ribbon.

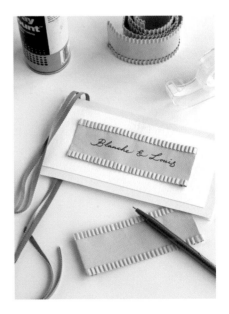

Blanche & Louis

...ome to our Wedding Party

...9th April 2~9 pm

...h Mews,

...5TE

3 For the written invitation cut the white watercolor paper using the craft knife and ruler so that it will slot into the front pocket. Using a thick embroidery needle pierce two holes in the top right-hand corner of the card. Cut some heart shapes from the gold tissue paper and pierce each heart once, with the needle, to make them easy to thread without tearing.

4 Now write the invitation card using the nib pen and gold ink, first practicing on a spare card. Attach a pearl, a gold or silver heart, and a gold tissue paper heart to the gold thread. Use your imagination here, choose whatever combination looks prettiest. Pass the thread through the two holes in the card and knot loosely at the front, then slot into the front pocket of the invitation card.

HINT

There are many beautiful papers to be found in specialist paper shops but don't overlook papers that may at first seem mundane—brown wrapping paper, waxed parchment, or glassine. Search in antique or bric-à-brac markets and collectors' fairs. An old-fashioned haberdashery stall may have reels of ribbon still with their original brown paper linings—perhaps crimped or stamped with their color code. Seen with a fresh eye these modest papers have potential for creative and decorative uses and when combined with a new, pristine paper their quiet charm shines through.

Glassine Envelope

Glassine paper, the semi-transparent utility paper traditionally used to protect photographic negatives and to interleave the pages of photograph albums, is ideal for making these envelopes that give a tantalizing glimpse of the Wedding Party Invitation within. Glassine cuts and folds beautifully and provides a perfect backdrop for a cascade of delicate paper hearts and a pearl trinket suspended on golden thread.

Materials

40gsm plain glassine paper
Selection of gold tissue papers
Vintage gold thread
Pearls
Gold hearts and charms
Cutting board
Craft knife
Metal safety ruler
Pencil
Bone folder
Scissors
Spray adhesive
Sharp darning needle

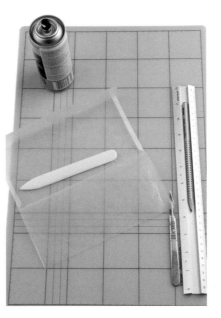

1 Using the template on page 142 as a guide, cut out an envelope from the glassine paper to 10in (25cm) long, using the ruler, pencil, cutting board, and craft knife. Working with the wrong side of the paper facing you, use the bone folder to make creases along the fold marks as indicated on the template, folding toward you. Spray the two side flaps, on the right side of the paper, with the spray adhesive, first being careful to mask off the surrounding areas, so that they are not also covered. Don't use general purpose glue as the glassine will pucker. Fold the bottom flap upward over the side flaps to form the envelope.

2 Assemble a selection of gold tissue papers and cut out small heart shapes using the scissors. Pierce each one with the darning needle to make them easy to thread. With the darning needle make two holes ¼in (5mm) apart in the flap of the envelope, ⅜in (1cm) from the bottom edge and centered in the width. Use a sharp needle so that the paper doesn't tear. Thread the darning needle with the gold thread and attach a tissue paper heart, a gold heart or charm, and a pearl. Choose any selection that looks suitably pretty. Now thread this once through the two holes in the envelope flap and tie at the front, with a knot or bow, on the outside.

2

The Bridal Shower

This gathering for the bride-to-be is the perfect occasion to evoke a truly feminine and glamorous atmosphere. For these adorable decorations—an invitation to the party, a gift handbag, cute crackers and fans, and a medley of delicious chocolate bars—simply choose the softest shades of a favorite color and add silken ribbons, a glint of gold, and a dash of black and white. What more could a girl possibly want?

Floral Invitations and Envelope

Gorgeous images of flowers in delicious hues of lilac, violet, and aquamarine are lined with sophisticated black and white to create these floral envelopes and invitations, both encircled with graceful ribbons.

Materials

Colored photocopies
Black and white photocopies
Thin ribbon
Cutting board
Craft knife
Metal safety ruler
Pencil
Bone folder
Scissors
Spray adhesive
Double-sided tape
Black rollerball pen

1 Make a selection of A4 color and black and white photocopies of pretty flower images taken from magazines or photographs, selecting images that match your chosen color scheme. Using the template on page 128 as a guide, cut out an envelope from one of the colored photocopies, to a length of 10in (25cm). With the wrong side facing you, use a bone folder to crease the paper at the fold points as marked on the template, folding toward you. For the lining of the envelope, using the same template, cut from a black and white photocopy.

2 Glue the wrong side of the black and white lining paper using spray adhesive and place this exactly over the envelope, wrong sides together, pressing to fix in place. Glue the two side flaps with spray adhesive, on the colored side of the paper, first masking off surrounding areas. To form the envelope, fold the bottom flap upward and press in position against the two side flaps.

3 At this point, use double-sided tape along the top edge of the envelope and fold over by ⅝in (1.5cm) to form a flap. Before sticking, take a 40in (1m) length of thin ribbon, fold this in two and center the folded end underneath the top flap. Now fold the flap over and press to fix.

4 To create the invitation, cut out a 3½ x 7in (9 x 18cm) rectangle from the floral black and white photocopy paper and a 7in (18cm) square of tracing paper and fold this in half to make a rectangle 3½ x 7in (9 x 18cm).

5 Now write your invitation on the front flap of the tracing paper with the black pen and tip in the black and white photocopy. Encircle this several times with thin ribbon and tie, then insert into the envelope.

HINT
Photocopying photographs or illustrations, first in color and then in black and white, is a quick and simple way to achieve inspirational imagery. Most photocopiers will take paper other than the standard as long as the weight and texture is correct for the machine, so try using an ivory 'laid' paper for a softer, more subtle effect. You can enlarge or reduce sections of an image and also adjust the color and tone settings, so just experiment until you have the desired effect.

Gift Handbags

These witty gift boxes, cleverly cut and shaped like little handbags, are reminiscent of the flirty fashion of the 1950s. The color scheme is continued in shades of lilac and aquamarine card and they can be constructed in differing sizes to accommodate a few delicious chocolates or a small gift. Each is customized with a chic grosgrain bow, a pretty initial, a floral lining, and a card or ribbon handle.

Materials

- 220gsm colored card
- Colored photocopies
- Grosgrain ribbon
- Thin satin ribbon
- Tracing paper
- Cutting board
- Craft knife
- Metal safety ruler
- Pencil
- Bone folder
- Scissors
- Double-sided tape
- Spray adhesive
- Hole punch

1 Using the template on page 129 as a guide, cut out the handbag from colored card, to fit either an A4 or A3 size, using the ruler, pencil, cutting board, and craft knife. Cut slit as marked, for the front fastening. With the bone folder, and the wrong side of the card facing you, crease along the fold marks as indicated on the template, turning the card toward you. Also crease the side pleats as marked on the template.

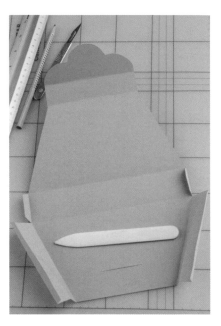

2 For the optional lining to the handbag, photocopy a picture of a favourite flower from a magazine or photograph, choosing an image that matches the color of the handbag. Glue the wrong side of the photocopy, using the spray adhesive, and position over the top half of the handbag with wrong sides together. Press in place. Cut around the outer edge of the photocopy, using the craft knife and cutting board, closely following the outer edge of the bag.

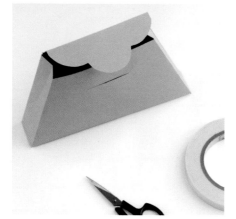 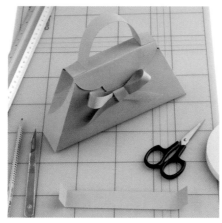 

3 To form the handbag shape, start with the inside of the bag facing you. Cut double-sided tape and attach it to the side flaps, on the right side of the card. Fold the front flap upward to join up to the side flaps and press in place. Crease the side pleats once again to give the handbag its shape. Fold the lid over to fasten through the front slit.

4 Using the template on page 129 to fit, cut out the handle, using the ruler, pencil, cutting board, and craft knife. Fold the handle as marked on the template at each end and fasten to the lid of the handbag using double-sided tape. Make a grosgrain bow, matching the ribbon color to the bag. Attach it to the front of the bag, just below the front slit, with a small piece of double-sided tape.

5 For an alternative handle, use a hole punch to make a hole in each side of the lid, as marked on the template. Thread a length of grosgrain ribbon, the same color as the front bow, through each hole and knot each end on the inside of the bag. Grosgrain ribbon is a good choice here because it holds its shape well.

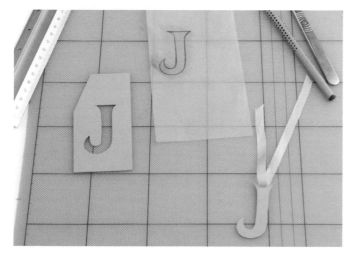 

6 To decorate the handbag with initials, trace a guest's initial from a typographic book or magazine, or simply design the letter yourself. Copy this on to tracing paper with a pencil. Turn the tracing paper over, wrong side towards you, and scribble over the surface with the pencil. Turn it back again and place it wrong side down onto a piece of colored card. Follow the outline of the letter using the pencil, pressing down firmly, so that the outline of the letter appears on the colored card. Cut out the shape using a cutting board and scalpel or scissors. Make a small slit at the top and thread the thin satin ribbon through it. Tie to the handle of the bag.

HINT

An invaluable source of inspiration, visual reference for typography can be found in printers' manuals, type books, manuscripts, and, of course, on your computer. Letters and numerals always have appeal and can be used in many new creative contexts. However, the mix of straight lines and curves can be tricky to cut so always use small craft scissors, or even embroidery scissors, to manage the curves and serifs. If you do decide to use a craft knife make sure the blade has some flexibility and use with great care. For ease, choose a typeface design that will be relatively straightforward to cut.

Party Fans

Translucent fans pleated neatly from tracing paper, edged with a black and white floral border and bound with slender ribbons, form a striking display when placed in elegant champagne or martini glasses.

Materials

90gsm tracing paper

Black and white photocopies

Thin ribbon

Cutting board

Craft knife

Metal safety ruler

Pencil

Bone folder

Scissors

Spray adhesive

Black rollerball pen

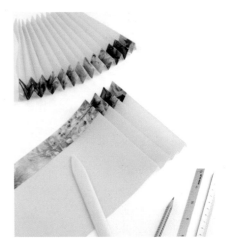

1 Make a black and white photocopy of a flower image then cut out two 1¼ x 10¼in (3 x 26cm) strips using the ruler, pencil, cutting board, and craft knife. Cut tracing paper to 6 x 20½in (15 x 52cm) and fix the strips along the top edge by glueing the wrong sides with spray adhesive.

2 To fold the fan, use the pencil and ruler to lightly mark out ¾in (2cm) intervals along the length of the tracing paper and score with the bone folder and ruler. Fold each crease firmly, the opposite way each time. With the right side facing, the first and last pleats should be folding away from you.

3 Once finished, press the creases very firmly in place. Wrap with thin ribbon, to hold the base of the fan in shape. As decoration, and as a gift to each of your guests, add a pendant or pair of earrings, threaded through the ribbon and tied.

4 Cut out 1⅜ x 6¼in (3.5 x 16cm) rectangles of photocopied paper and tracing paper. Fold both in half then fit the tracing paper with the guest's name inside. To hold the sheets in place, pierce a small hole through the papers and loop with an earring or pendant.

Chocolate Bar Wraps

Why not enhance the floral theme with your own beautifully-dressed chocolate bars? Simply create stylish 'wraps' from photocopied flower images and add chic paper bows in a medley of pretty colors. These will make fitting mementos for a special party, and prove that a most charming result can emerge from the simplest of ideas.

Materials

Chocolate bars
Colored photocopies
120gsm colored paper
Cutting board
Craft knife
Metal safety ruler
Pencil
Scissors
Double-sided tape

1 Make a selection of colored A4 photocopies from favorite flower pictures taken from magazines or photographs, choosing images that match your chosen color scheme. Using the ruler, pencil, cutting board, and craft knife cut out rectangles from this floral paper to the length of your chocolate bar, and long enough to wrap completely around. Overlap by ⅜in (1cm) at the back and fasten with double-sided tape. You can use any size chocolate bars but try to find ones that already have a gold or silver inner wrapper.

2 To make the band for a chocolate bar 3½in (9cm) long, cut a strip of a matching colored paper ⅝in (1.5cm) wide and long enough to wrap round the middle of the bar, with a small overlap at the back. Use a strip of double-sided tape to fasten. For the flat bow, cut a strip of the same paper ⅝ x 6in (1.5 x 15cm), fold each end into the middle, and secure with a small piece of double-sided tape. Wrap a smaller strip of paper ⅝ x 1⅝in (1.5 x 4cm) around the join, and stick at the back. Attach this bow at the front of the band with double-sided tape. Larger bars of chocolate can be wrapped in the same way, just modify the measurements.

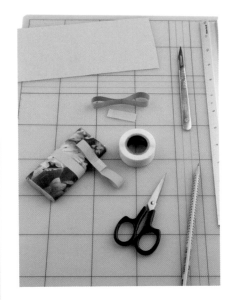

Bonbon Crackers

These sweetest of crackers are made from pure white crepe paper decorated with a glint of gold doily edging, a floral band and fragile flowers of tissue paper. Pile them on a silver tray to delight your guests.

Materials

220gsm white card
White crepe paper
Colored photocopies
Lilac tissue paper
Floristry wire or store-bought
  stems
Gold doily paper
Cutting board
Craft knife
Metal safety ruler
Pencil
Scissors
Double-sided tape
Vintage gold thread
Darning needle
Multi-purpose adhesive

1 To make the inner tube, cut thin white card to 3½ x 5½in (9 x 14cm) and curve into a tube. Overlap by ⅜in (1cm) and secure with double-sided tape. Cut a length of white crepe paper 10 x 20in (25 x 50cm) and decorate both long sides with thin strips of gold doily paper, using only the scalloped edge. With narrow strips of double-sided tape, glue the gold strips to the edge of the crepe, so that only ⅛in (2mm) of gold shows. Only decorate about 8in (20cm) along the edge as the rest will not show.

2 Roll the crepe around the tube with the gold edge showing. Secure it with double-sided tape. Twist one end of the crepe, tie with gold thread, and knot. Fill the cracker with bonbons or a motto, then twist and tie the other end. For the band, photocopy a pretty flower image and cut to 2¾ x 6in (7 x 15cm), decorate the two longest sides with the scalloped edges from the gold doily paper as Step 1. Wrap this around the cracker, securing it with double-sided tape.

3 Cut out simple flower shapes from the tissue paper. Pierce the center of each flower with a darning needle. Using a 2in (5cm) length of floristry wire or a store-bought stem, turn over the top of the stem by about ⅛in (2mm). Gather three or four layers of petals together and thread on to the stem, positioning at the turned end. Fix in position with a spot of glue. When completely dry, pinch each flower slightly at the base to give it shape. Thread one under each floral band.

3

The Wedding Table

Welcoming friends and family to the celebration, however elaborate or simple, signifies the joy of the occasion. Here, imaginative details and inspirational finishing touches highlight the romantic ambience of the day, showing how an original but relaxed approach can be charming, and create that vital first impression as your guests arrive. By using such elements as an elegant script, a cluster of translucent leaves, or just the simplest daisy decoration, a beautiful style evolves.

Decorated Table Planner

A seating plan is vital to help your guests find their table. This stylish idea of cards featuring their names printed in a classic italic script with flashes of gold in the hand-lettered table numbers and in the decorations of vintage buttons and earrings, is easily adapted to suit either a formal or more relaxed setting.

Materials

Gold polyethylene synthetic
　material or gold wrapping
　paper
¼in (5mm) thick polyboard
Thin white card
Ivory 'laid' paper suitable for
　computer printing
Vintage gold thread
Gold and glass buttons
Vintage braid
Vintage gold earrings
Vintage gold ribbon
Cutting board
Craft knife
Metal safety ruler
Pencil
Scissors
Double-sided tape
Adhesive tape
Spray adhesive
Multi-purpose adhesive
Gold marker pen (extra-fine
　point)

1 This planner has room for 9 tables so increase or reduce the dimensions if you need to accommodate a different number. With pencil, ruler, craft knife, and cutting board, cut a sheet of polyboard 23½ x 15in (60 x 38cm). Then cut the gold synthetic material or wrapping paper to 30 x 21in (76 x 53cm). Glue the reverse side of the gold paper using the spray adhesive, then position the polyboard in the middle of the paper and press together to adhere. Turn the edges over the polyboard, folding the corners as if wrapping a parcel. Add extra adhesive if necessary. Smooth out any creases that may appear on the front.

2 Cut a length of gold braid the width of the board plus approximately 1½in (4cm) each side for turning. Back this with double-sided tape. With the right side of the table planner facing you, position the trim along the bottom edge, turning the excess around to the back at each end. With pencil and ruler, measure out the position where each tag will hang and mark this by gluing on a button with multi-purpose adhesive.

3 Using the pencil, ruler, craft knife, and cutting board, cut out nine tags 4¾ x 2⅜in (12 x 6cm) from the white card. On a computer type out a list of six guests for each tag and print on to ivory paper using a classic italic font. Cut these into 4¾ x 2⅜in (12 x 6cm) rectangles, with the names centered horizontally, leaving enough space at the bottom for the table number. Spray the reverse side of the paper with adhesive and glue each onto a tag. At the bottom write the relevant table number with a gold marker pen.

4 To hang each tag, cut a piece of gold thread approximately 4in (10cm) long. Double this over and glue at the back of the tag, at the top edge, with adhesive tape. Decorate each tag with a gold earring simply clipped over the top edge.

HINT
A classic script printed in black onto cream or ivory paper has a timeless appeal but to achieve a more luxurious 'baroque' feel combine with the sheen of gold or silver. Browse in local flea markets and antique stalls and look for wooden spools of metallic embroidery thread traditionally used in 'haute couture' fashion and religious or military regalia. Lengths of intricate braid and gleaming buttons are fascinating and inexpensive to collect. Vintage earrings, even if not part of a pair, are useful as they can be simply clipped onto card or paper to decorate and add beguiling gleam.

5 To hang the table planner, or for decoration, cut a length of gold ribbon and attach it to the top edge, on the reverse side. Glue in position with double-sided tape and reinforce with a strip of gold paper if necessary. Now, hang a tag to each button starting with table number 1.

Wish Tree

This lovely idea takes inspiration from a Dutch tradition. Pendants of watercolor paper, each lettered with a guest's name, are decorated with translucent and textured paper leaves threaded through ribbons and draped over a champagne glass to designate their place at the wedding table. Each person writes a wish to the bride and groom on the back of the pendant and ties it to a slender branch so creating a striking display.

Materials

150gsm watercolor paper
88gsm Japanese Kyoseishi
   bleached white paper
21gsm Japanese Rakusui Lace
   Flocked paper tissue
Green silk paper
40gsm linen-look glassine
   paper
40gsm plain glassine paper
90 or 112gsm tracing paper
Selection of slender ribbons,
   40in (1 m) per pendant
Gold or silver marker pen
   (extra-fine point)
Hole punch
Cutting board
Craft knife
Metal safety ruler
Pencil
Scissors
Double-sided tape

1 For the hanging pendants, with a ruler and pencil, cutting board, and craft knife, cut rectangles of watercolor paper 1⅝ x 8⅝in (4 x 22cm). Make a hole at one end with the hole punch, about ⅜in (1cm) in from the edge. Use a marker pen to write the name of one guest on one side of each of the rectangular pendants. Leave the other side blank for your guest to write their 'wish' for the bride and the groom.

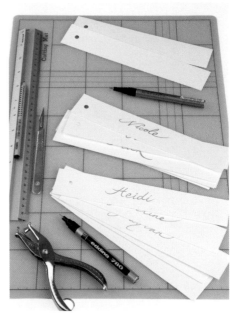

2 Gather together a selection of white papers mixing translucent papers with Kyoseishi textured paper. Include an accent color if required, in this case a green silk paper. With scissors or craft knife cut out the leaf shapes from the templates on page 130. Punch a hole at the base of each leaf about ⅜in (1cm) in from the end. Crease each leaf down its length, to give it extra form.

3 Select a mixture of 4 or 5 leaves for each cluster and one pendant, then thread them together with ribbon. Tie a loose half-knot at the base of each cluster. Place one leaf and pendant cluster for each guest at the wedding table along with a silver pen so that they can write a 'wish' on the back. The guest will then tie their 'wish' to a branch of the Wish Tree with the ribbon.

4 For an alternative color scheme, write the name of each guest with gold marker pen and choose soft pink, taupe, coffee, and ivory ribbons for each leaf cluster, making sure to only use white leaves.

HINT
Translucent paper can create especially beautiful wedding decorations when you want to achieve a delicate and ethereal effect. You can use utility papers such as glassine and tracing paper as well as the decorative papers like Japanese Rakusui (with gaps on the surface created by dropping water) and Japanese Unryu (with embedded silk fibres). Thai silk papers, in beautiful jewel-like colors, are also useful.
Fine papers are tricky to cut especially with a craft knife so try laying a firmer, opaque paper underneath and secure with masking tape before you start.

Decorated Name Cards

These elegant name cards are perfect to denote the guest's place at the table and will make everyone feel welcome. Using a beautiful italic script with a hint of a flourish printed on to an ivory 'laid' paper, each one is decorated with intricate braid, a loop of golden thread, and a lustrous pearl to reflect the romance of the day.

Materials

Thin white card
Ivory 'laid' paper suitable for
 computer printing
Vintage gold thread
Vintage gold braid
Decorative pearls
Cutting board
Craft knife
Metal safety ruler
Pencil
Scissors
Spray adhesive
Double-sided tape

1 With ruler, pencil, craft knife, and cutting board, cut out name cards 2⅜ x 4¾in (6 x 12cm) from the white card. Type out each guest's name on a computer, and print out on the ivory paper using a large italic script. Cut to the size of the card, with the name positioned exactly in the middle. Glue on the wrong side of the paper with spray adhesive, position carefully and fix to the card.

2 For the loop, cut a 3in (7.5cm) length of gold thread, double it over and attach it to the back of the card, on the left-hand edge with a tiny strip of double-sided tape. Cut a 4¾in (12cm) strip of the gold braid, back it with double-sided tape, and fix it to the front of the name card allowing 1¼in (3cm) of braid each side to be folded over to the back of the card, covering the ends of the loop. For extra decoration, with a length of thread tie a pearl to the loop so that it hangs loosely at the front of the name card.

Souvenir Wallets

It is the imaginative details that add to the ambience of the wedding table. Little wallets of old-gold moiré tissue paper—reminiscent of silk taffeta—are softly padded, folded, and decorated with lustrous pearls. They are the perfect size to contain within the pocket a black and white photo, a name-card, and a few sugared almonds.

Materials

Gold moiré patterned tissue
  paper
White tissue paper
Vintage gold thread
Decorative pearls
Cutting board
Craft knife
Metal safety ruler
Pencil
Scissors
Double-sided tape
Spray adhesive

1 With ruler, pencil, cutting board, and craft knife, cut out the gold moiré tissue paper to 7½ x 14½in (19 x 37cm). Cut out the white tissue paper, 8 or 10 sheets thick, to 6¼ x 13¾in (16 x 35cm) . If you can't find the beautiful, moiré-patterned, printed tissue paper used here, then use ordinary gold tissue paper.

2 Working with the wrong side of the gold tissue paper facing you, fold in the edges all around by ⅝in (1.5cm) on the longest sides and ⅜in (1cm) on the short sides. Line inside the folds with double-sided tape, and place the layers of white tissue paper within the folds. Turn over the edges, peel back the double-sided tape, and glue onto the white tissue, folding in neatly at each corner as if wrapping a parcel.

3 Cut a 2in (5cm) length of gold thread and loop this through a pearl. Double over the thread and position at the center of one end, on the wrong side of the paper. Fasten with a strip of double-sided tape. To line the wallet, cut another rectangle of gold tissue paper 6 x 13¾in (15 x 35cm). Spray this on the wrong side with adhesive and carefully position over the wrong side of the wallet, covering the white tissue paper.

4 With the inside of the wallet facing you, form the pocket by folding over the end opposite the pearl, by 2¾in (7cm). Glue with thin strips of double-sided tape down each side of the pocket, on the inside, first cutting the tape to a width of ¼in (5mm). Now evenly fold the wallet twice, ending with the pearl at the front.

HINT
For wedding decorations, gold and silver tissue papers are particularly useful, as their metallic luster compliments perfectly sparkling glassware, beautiful cutlery and antique or modern candlesticks. You can easily strengthen these fragile papers by padding with layers of ordinary white tissue paper, and then enhance the luxurious effect with vintage embroidery thread and graceful pearl droplets. Just look in bric-à-brac markets for pretty pearls, maybe from broken pendants, earrings or bracelets—a small collection will prove invaluable to embellish many paper projects.

Table Centerpiece

A charmingly original table centerpiece is created from paper leaves featuring intriguing scripts and handwriting from love notes and letters. Leaves cut from translucent papers give extra definition to the array when all are wired onto a beribboned hoop.

Materials

Cable wire ⅛in (3mm) diameter

Photocopied typographic
  papers

Translucent papers—90gsm
  Pergamenata, 47gsm
  Japanese Rayon Unryu

White ribbon 80 in (2m) length,
  ½in (1.5cm) wide

Wire cutters

Scissors

Double-sided tape

Adhesive tape

Silver jewelry wire

Fine gold beading wire

White acrylic paint

Fine paintbrush

Caution: Never leave a lit candle unattended and always extinguish after use.

1 For the base of the centerpiece, use the wire cutters to cut a 35in (90cm) length of wire and twist it to form a circle. Overlap the ends of the wire by about ¾in (2cm) and secure at this point with silver jewelry wire.

2 Wrap the wire with white ribbon, first securing it to the wire with a strip of double-sided tape. When completely covered, secure the ribbon at the end, again with double-sided tape, and trim off any excess ribbon.

3 Collect together a selection of typography from books, magazines, and hand-written love letters. Include as many decorative typefaces as you can find. Photocopy these onto white or ivory paper. From these cut out leaf shapes to a variety of sizes using the templates on page 130. Cut out more leaves from the translucent papers also using the templates. Fold each leaf down its length to give it form.

Paper-dressed Bride

A small doll, clothed in delicate papers—a petticoat of tissue, a gown of crepe, a veil of sheer Hakuryu paper—and holding the sweetest paper and pearl bouquet becomes a beautiful and special centerpiece for the bridesmaids' table.

Materials

7in (18cm) tall doll
White crepe paper
White tissue paper
7.5gsm Japanese Hakuryu fine
   white paper
White satin ribbon
Gold thread
Metal safety ruler
Pencil
Spray adhesive
Darning needle
White cotton thread
Scissors

For the flowers:
88gsm Japanese Kyoseishi
   bleached white paper
Green silk paper
Silver beading wire
Pearls
Thin white ribbon
Multi-purpose adhesive
Double-sided tape
Scissors
Darning needle

1 Using the templates on page 131 as a guide, cut out the petticoat from tissue paper, the dress from crepe paper, and the veil from sheer Hakuryu paper with scissors. Adjust the sizes to fit your doll. With needle and white thread, use tiny stitches, ½in (1cm) in from the top edge of the tissue paper, to gather the waist of the petticoat to fit the waist of your doll. Do the same with the dress but the stitches should be closer, only ⅛in (3mm) from the top edge. At the center point of the veil, as marked on the template, make four tiny pleats, close together, using the needle and white thread and tiny stitches.

2 Add a simple bodice of white satin ribbon around the doll and sew at the back with needle and white thread. Attach the tissue petticoat to the waist of the doll, and fasten at the back with two or three stitches. Close up the back seam with very thin strips of double-sided tape. Attach the crepe dress over the top of the petticoat, positioning it over the satin bodice. Using the needle and thread, fasten the dress at the back with two or three stitches. Use very thin strips of double-sided tape to close up the back seam. Secure the dress by winding gold thread around eight or nine times, covering the white gathered stitches, and tying in a tiny bow at the back. Attach the veil to the top of the doll's head, using a small piece of double-sided tape underneath the pleats.

Cake Decorations

Daisy-shaped flowers cut from pure white Japanese Kyoseishi paper are so simple to make. This paper, made from the Kozo or Mulberry plant, is strong and flexible and has a striking 'crushed' texture which compliments the smoothness of the icing. The flowers are embellished with delicate pearl and gilt centers.

Materials

White Japanese Kyoseishi
  paper
Decorative pearls
Scissors
Silver beading wire
Darning needle

1 Cut small circles of Kyoseishi paper with scissors approximately 1¼in (3cm) in diameter. Cut out daisy-shaped flowers from the circles or use the template on page 131. It doesn't matter if they are all slightly different, this will only add to their charm. If you can't find this Japanese paper, look for something unusual that is as white as possible with an interesting texture.

2 Pierce the center of each flower with the darning needle. Cut beading wire 3in (7.5cm) long. Thread through the center of a pearl by about ¾in (2cm), turn over this short end of wire and thread back through the pearl. Pull gently so that the bend of the wire holds the pearl. Thread a flower onto the wire, passing both thicknesses of wire through the hole made by the darning needle. To hold the flower in place twist the short end of the wire into a tight circle underneath the flower. Insert the flower stems into the cake to decorate. Never use glue near edible products, as it could be poisonous.

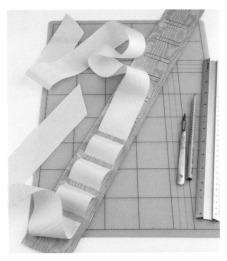

4 Work with the wrong side of the rectangle facing you. Using the pencil and ruler, mark out where each slit will go. With craft knife and cutting board for a ribbon 2in (5cm) wide start 2in (5cm) in from one end marking out slits 2in (5cm) deep x ⅛in (1mm) wide at intervals of ⅜in (1cm) and 1⅝in (4cm), repeated from the first slit, leaving the last 2in (5cm) of rectangle uncut. Thread the ribbon through.

5 With the extra-strength all-purpose adhesive, glue around the inside of the box base at the rim where the two ovals meet. Position the bottom, inside edge of the box side against the glued rim and press until the glue has dried. Ensure the loose ribbon is at the front of the box with the two ends of box sides overlapping. Glue the overlap with more adhesive. When dry, tie the ribbon into a bow and trim the ends diagonally.

6 For the box lid, using pencil, cutting board, and craft knife, cut out an oval from the mount board 9in (23cm) long, and cover with tissue, following the instructions in Step 1. On the wrong side of the oval, make a slit in the middle 1¼in (3cm) deep and ⅛in (2mm) wide. Cut another smaller oval 7⅞in (20cm) long, and cover this with tissue, again as in Step 1.

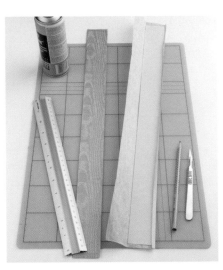

7 Fold the 6in (15cm) length of the 1¼in (3cm) wide ribbon in two and thread the two loose ends through the slit in the oval, so that a loop of ribbon shows on the right side, and ¾in (2cm) of each end is on the wrong side. Secure the loose ends with double-sided tape. Glue the smaller oval to the larger oval, as in Step 2.

8 For the lid sides, using pencil, ruler, cutting board, and craft knife, cut out a 1⅝ x 22in (4 x 56cm) strip of card and a 3½ x 23in (9 x 58cm) strip of tissue paper. Using spray adhesive, glue the wrong side of the tissue and cover the card, as in Step 3.

9 To form the lid, glue the sides to the inside of the oval lid at the rim, following the instructions in Step 5. Glue the two overlapping sides together with all-purpose adhesive. For the almond box, which has no lid, just adapt the measurements of the box sides to fit a 1¼in (3cm) wide ribbon, making a shallower box. The base for both versions is identical.

4

Accessories

Myriad papers—ethereal, textured, softly-patterned, and painted—
ensures every thoughtful token of your wedding day is beautifully
dressed! The time spent creating these inspirational accessories, some
so simple and others a little more complicated, will guarantee to
enchant and impress. As always, it is the tiny details that make the
difference—a pearl against burnished gold paper or a faceted glass
button on a paper flower.

3 To make quick pom-poms for the center of each flower, cut out a 1⅝ x 4in (4 x 10cm) rectangle of card. Wrap the wool around the card until it is full. With a needle, thread a length of the wool between the wool and the card, then detach the needle and tie the two ends of wool tightly, gathering up all the wool. Cut through the wool on the opposite side of the card, releasing the wrapped wool into a pom-pom and trim if necessary.

4 To decorate the flower, glue the pom-pom into the center of the petals, using adhesive. Choose a bead, button, or earring and glue firmly into the center of the pom-pom, fluffing up the wool strands slightly. Wrap your gift in white crepe paper and wrap a length of silk ribbon around the outside. Now attach the flower to the ribbon using double-sided tape or, alternatively, at a jaunty angle in the corner of your gift.

HINT

Japanese Mitzutamashi papers have a quality reminiscent of lace fabric and are thus ideal for many wedding papercraft projects. The word literally means 'waterdrop paper' and it involves the technique of spraying or sprinkling water through a stencil. It is these differing stencil designs that determine the paper's final appearance, so you can find Mitzutamashi paper with, for example, fan, snowflake, square, or lace motifs. A variation on these is Rakasui decorative paper, which has a similar 'filigree' texture. Both types combine well with other papers such as crepe and tissue to create unusual and luxurious effects.

3 With scissors, cut a rectangle of Kyoseishi paper 2 x 4in (5 x 10cm). Glue one side with spray adhesive and press down firmly inside the base of the bag. Hold in position until dry. This will add extra firmness and help the bag hold its shape. At this point, crease the side pleats again to reinforce the shape of the bag.

4 Fold over the top flap of the bag and use the hole punch to punch a hole ¾in (2cm) from the bottom edge of the flap and centered in the width, as marked on the template, making sure to punch the hole through all three thicknesses of paper. Fill the favor bags and close the flap, then thread a length of grosgrain ribbon through the holes and tie loosely at the front.

HINT

It is the texture that distinguishes and gives the unique quality to the different types of paper available. From the crumpled 'elephant hide' of Nepalese Lokta and the soft crushed texture of Japanese Kyoseishi, to the smooth sheen of Glassine and the imitation parchments such as Pergamenata. There are the Asian cotton rag Khadi papers and of course the varying surfaces of watercolor paper: from the smoothest hot pressed, through soft pressed, cold pressed, and rough, which has the most texture. Invaluable to use with fibrous and heavy decorative papers is a bone folder, which, when held against a ruler, makes precise creases in paper and gives a professional look to craft projects. Traditionally fashioned from bone, they also now come in man-made materials.

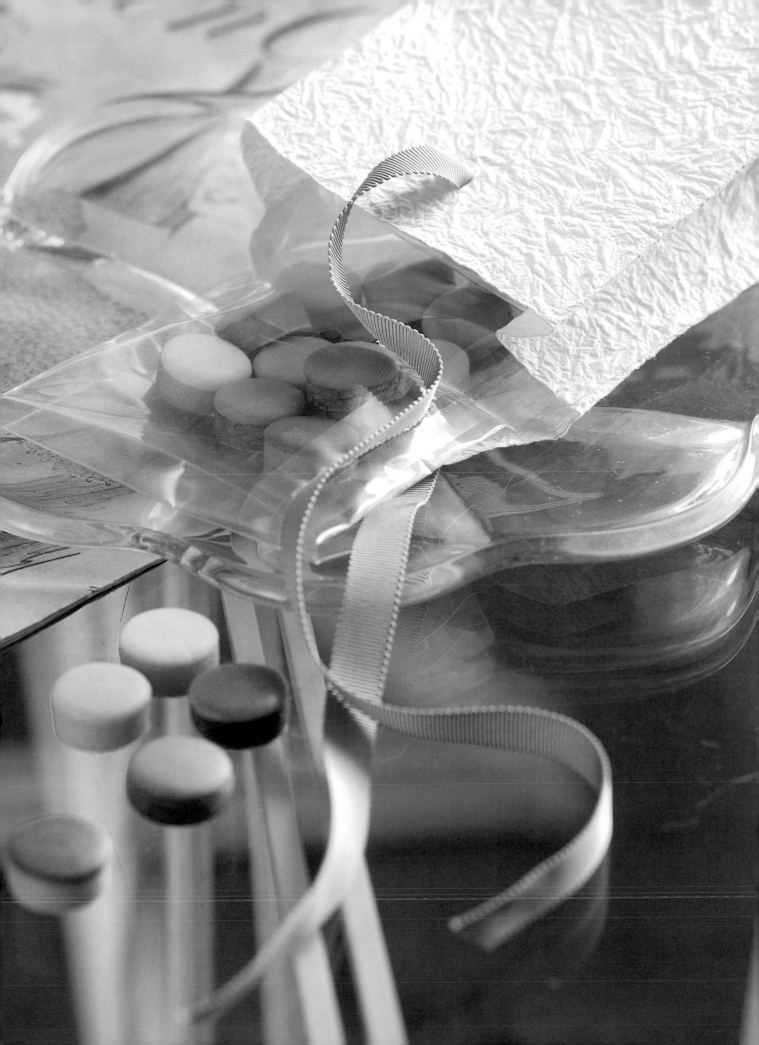

Patterned Confetti Boxes

Cute confetti boxes of softly-patterned wallpapers, are punched and beribboned, and filled to the brim with tissue paper petals. In silvers, creams, and pinks they form a harmonious array.

Materials

Selection of patterned
  wallpaper samples or off-cuts
  ⅛in (2mm) thick white mount
  card
20in (50cm) length of ½in
  (1.5cm) wide colored ribbon
Colored tissue papers
Silver ¼in (5mm) eyelet and
  washer kit
Small hammer
Cutting board
Craft knife
Metal safety ruler
Pencil
Compass
Hole punch
Scissors
Multi-purpose adhesive

Wallpaper: Bovary Collection at
www.ninacampbell.com

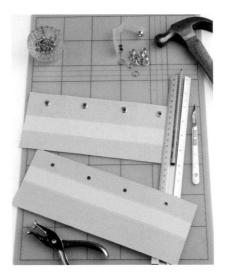

1 With ruler, pencil, craft knife, and cutting board, cut out the wallpaper to a rectangle 4 x 10¼in (10 x 26cm). With the right side of the paper facing you, with a pencil and ruler mark four points along the rectangle for the holes, ¾in (2cm) down from the top edge. Each hole should be spaced evenly apart when the box is completed. Punch all four holes with the hole punch. Using an eyelet and washer kit, follow the instructions given to fit an eyelet in each hole. You will need a small hammer to close the eyelets once they are in place.

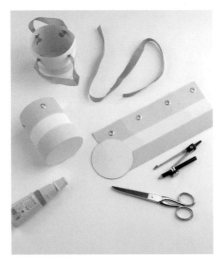

2 With the compass and pencil mark a circle 3⅛in (8cm) in diameter on the card. Cut out with scissors. Apply multi-purpose adhesive along the bottom ⅛in (2mm) inside edge of the wallpaper and around the outer edge of the card circle, wrap the wallpaper around the circle and hold in place until the adhesive is dry. Glue where the seam overlaps. Cut two lengths of ribbon 10in (25cm) long, thread each end through a hole and knot on the inside to secure.

3 For the confetti, gather together a selection of colored tissue papers to match the color of the confetti boxes. With the scissors, cut out simple heart shapes in multiples by making a wad of ten or more sheets of tissue paper and cutting through the layers. Mix up the colored heart shapes and fill each box.

Bridesmaid's Headband

The light filters through the fairy-tale blooms formed from translucent decorative Japanese and burnished gold Asian papers. A few gathered together on a slender headband is undeniably charming.

Materials

7.5gsm white Japanese
   Hakuryu paper
White Japanese Rakasui lace
   flocked paper
20gsm white Japanese Rakasui
   lace laid paper
Gold Asian synthetic woven
   sheet paper, silk paper, or
   25gsm Asarakusui paper
Floristry wire or store-bought
   stems
Pearls
White satin-covered headband
Cutting board
Craft knife
Metal safety ruler
Pencil
Scissors
Multi-purpose adhesive

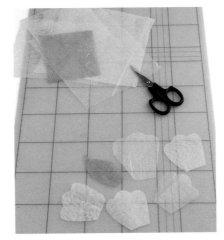

1 With scissors, using the template on page 136 as a guide, cut out flower petals from squares of the fine white Japanese papers. Make larger petals approximately 3⅛in (8cm) long, and smaller petals 2⅜in (6cm) long. Cut a few leaves from the gold paper about 3½in (9cm) long.

2 For the stems, cut floristry wire or store-bought stems, into 3½in (9cm) lengths. Collect together a selection of pearls of different sizes. Thread a pearl onto a stem, first adding a spot of multi-purpose adhesive to secure.

3 Crease each petal at its base, dab with adhesive to hold the crease and allow to dry. Glue the petals and wrap each one around the stem, just below the pearl. Overlap them until you have a flower of nine petals, less for a bud. Glue gold leaves on the outside.

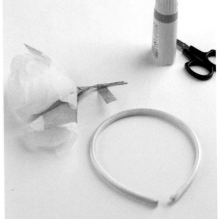

4 Gather two or more flowers together and bind them with a strip of gold paper ⅜ x 2⅜in (1 x 6cm) long, lightly covered on one side with glue and wrapped around the stems. Position the flowers on the headband, slightly to one side and glue to secure.

5

The Children's Table

To create a design theme for your young guests is a charming thought and is so easily translated to their own special invitations, table settings, and wedding favors, but always complimenting the main ambience of the wedding party. The key ingredients are simplicity itself—motifs of leaves, blossoms, birds, and butterflies, all cut from the prettiest pastel-colored matt, translucent, and pearlized papers.

3 For the inner lining, using pencil, ruler, craft knife, and cutting board, cut out the Pergamenata paper to 5½ x 15in (14 x 38cm), score down the center with the bone folder and fold in half. To secure the inner lining within the invitation card, glue about a ⅛in (3mm) along the folded edge of the Pergamenata paper with the spray adhesive, first masking off the surrounding areas. Tip the folded paper inside the invitation against the spine and press to fix it in place.

4 For the less detailed invitation enlarge the design on page 137 to 4½ x 8in (11.5 x 20cm) and follow the previous instructions, adjusting all the paper measurements. For both invitation designs, a simple way to cut the eye is to first make a tiny cross and then cut in quarter segments.

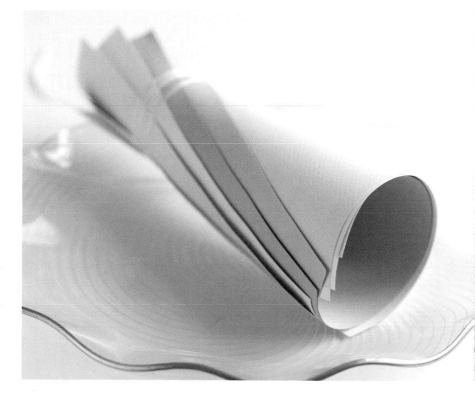

HINT

Papers in beautiful muted colors, as well as more intense hues, are stocked in all art and specialist paper stores. Papers that have a pattern of ribbed lines in the finished sheet are 'laid' papers—these have a matt, velvety texture and are invaluable as they give an understated elegance to any paper project. It is customary for the 'laid' lines to run across the width and the 'chain' lines to run head to foot as the mold used to make 'laid' paper has numerous narrowly spaced wires that are woven together by very thin wires or threads called chain lines.

Memories Album

Preserve your memories by compiling an enchanting, ribbon-bound album to hold the precious keepsakes and mementos relating to your wedding day and the preparation time beforehand. A swatch of silk-satin, a sample of tulle, a faded flower … all find safe haven within interleaving glassine pages.

Materials

300gsm watercolor paper
150gsm watercolor paper
Thin white card
40gsm glassine paper
80in (2m) length of 1in (2.5cm)
   wide ivory ribbon
16½in (42cm) length of ⅜in
   (1cm) wide ivory ribbon
Decorative sheets of lettering
   and vintage haberdashery
Cutting board
Craft knife
Metal safety ruler
Pencil
Scissors
Hole punch
Spray adhesive
Double-sided tape
Sample pots of matt emulsion
   paint
Artist's flat paintbrush

1 For the front and back album covers, use the pencil, ruler, craft knife, and cutting board to cut out two 12⅝ x 20in (32 x 50cm) rectangles from the 300gsm paper. Cut out an 4⅜ x 14⅛in (11 x 36cm) window centered visually on one of these rectangles. Cut out as many 12⅝ x 20in (32 x 50cm) pages from the 150gsm watercolor paper as you think you will need, remembering one of these will be used to back the 'windowed' front cover. With the hole punch, make four holes along the spine ¾in (2cm) in from the edge, identically positioned on each page and the cover. Cut out the same number of pages 12⅝ x 18½in (32 x 46.5cm) from the glassine paper.

2 To decorate the front cover paint eight rectangles of emulsion paint in toning shades on white card, each at least 4 x 3⅛in (10 x 8cm). Alternatively you can just buy colored card. When the paint is dry, cut eight 2⅜ x 1⅝in (6 x 4cm) rectangles from the painted card and punch a hole in each one, in the top right-hand corner. Decorate each card with a mixture of cut-out letters spelling the word LOVE, tiny buttons on a card, a piece of lace or tulle, to make a creative collage. Fix in position with double-sided tape.

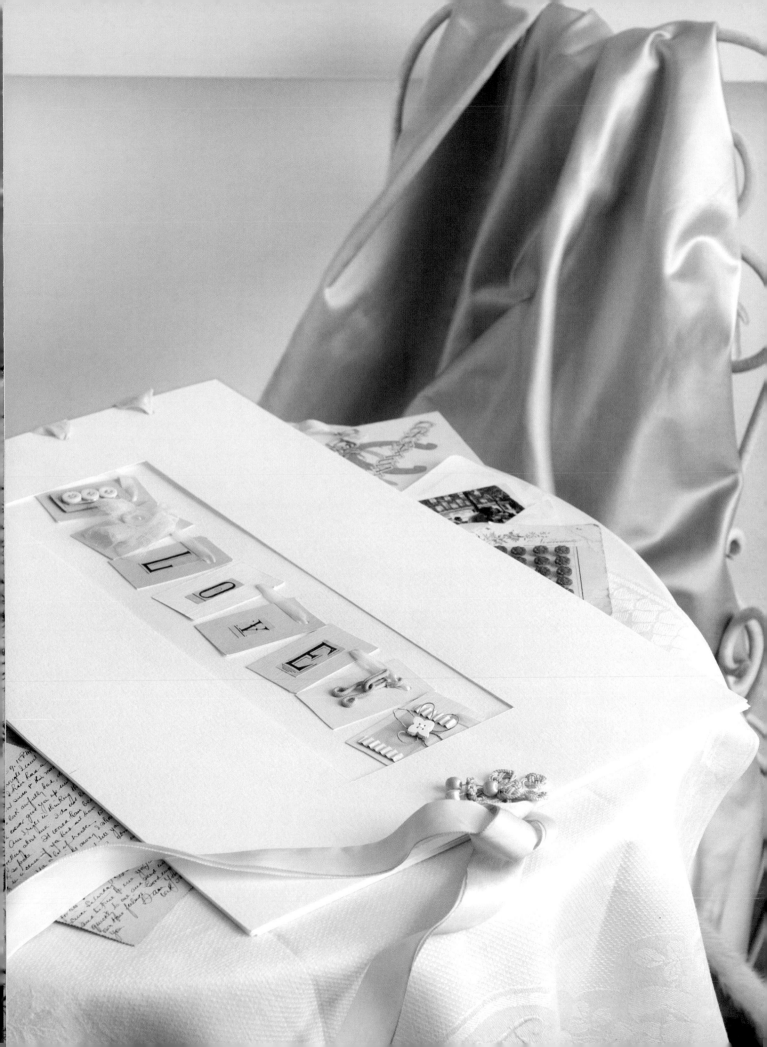

Keepsake Portfolio

A useful tie-up portfolio made from card and covered with a remnant of favorite wallpaper is somewhere special to place your valued documents and important correspondence. Alternatively, use it to store treasured mementos and keepsakes from your wedding day.

Materials

Wallpaper remnant—60in
  (1.5m) length
Cartridge paper
Cream paper
1/8in (2mm) thick mount board
100in (2.5m) length of 3/4in
  (2cm) wide ivory cotton tape
20in (50cm) length of linen
  bookbinding cloth
Cutting board
Craft knife
Metal safety ruler
Pencil
Bone folder
Hole punch
Spray adhesive
Double-sided tape
Multi-purpose adhesive
Scissors
Masking tape
Binders PVA paste and brush

Wallpaper: Lilac Trail at
www.colefax.com

1 For the front and back portfolio covers, using the pencil, ruler, craft knife, and cutting board, cut out two 12¾ x 18in (32.5 x 45cm) rectangles from the mount board and two 14¾ x 20in (37.5 x 50cm) rectangles from the wallpaper.

2 Cover the wrong side of one rectangle of wallpaper with spray adhesive and position the mount board accurately in the middle (if it has a gray side put this face down) and glue together. Fold the wallpaper edges over onto the mount board and glue in position. For neatness cut diagonal corners in the two uppermost folds.

3 Cut out the portfolio's three flaps from the wallpaper, two 5 x 10¾in (12.5 x 27cm) and the other 5 x 16⅝in (12.5 x 42cm). To strengthen the flaps line them with cartridge paper cut to the same size and glue together using spray adhesive. Score a line using a bone folder held against a ruler, along one side of each flap ⅝in (1.5cm) in and fold inward. Cut off the other corners diagonally.

4 Position the longest flap on the inside of a wallpapered rectangle, centered within the width with the scored ⅝in (1.5cm) edge folded flat and positioned about ¼in (5mm) from the outer edge. Glue this folded edge in position using spray adhesive or fix with double-sided tape. Repeat this procedure with the two shorter flaps. This now becomes the back of the folio.

5 Cut slits, slightly wider than the cotton tape, in the front and back boards using a craft knife, centered along the width of the two top edges and about 1in (2.5cm) in. Thread a 24in (60cm) length of cotton tape through each slit and glue the ends inside with multi-purpose adhesive. Glue a 24in (60cm) length of tape to the two smaller flaps centered along each width.

6 Cut a 2¾ x 19¼in (7 x 49cm) strip of bookbinding cloth with scissors and apply binder's paste in dabbing motions on the wrong side of the strip. Place the bottom edges of the folio centered on this strip leaving a 1in (2.5cm) gap between them. Press firmly to glue in position. Fold over the remainder of the cloth at both ends and press firmly to fix in place.

7 Cut two 12⅜ x 19¼in (31 x 43cm) rectangles from cream paper and, using spray adhesive on their reverse sides, glue them to the inside covers. Cut another 3⅛ x 19¼in (8 x 43cm) strip of bookbinding cloth to cover the join and glue using binder's paste applied with the brush. Press firmly to fix. Add a label to the front.

HINT

It is worthwhile keeping remnants and samples of wallpaper for many creative paper projects. There is a huge range of stunning patterns in both traditional and contemporary styles with many beautiful color schemes and gorgeous textures. The method of printing, often silkscreened, gives wallpaper a unique handmade quality which becomes an integral part of your paper designs. Depending on the project, wallpaper can be used on its own or to cover a base card or paper as it is both sturdy and flexible.

Thank You Folder

Personalize your thank-you notes, adding your own indelible style, with these simple tracing paper folders embellished with a rose cluster motif, a vintage glass button, and entwined gold thread. Each folder is lined with semi-translucent pages and contains a sweet matching envelope to hold a few thoughtful keepsakes and a handwritten note.

Materials

Color photocopies on 60gsm
  A4 tracing paper
90gsm Pergamenata or
  semi-translucent paper
Ivory 'laid' paper
Decorative images and
  photographs
Vintage gold thread
Vintage glass buttons
Cutting board
Craft knife
Metal safety ruler
Pencil
Bone folder
Scissors
Spray adhesive
Multi-purpose adhesive
Double-sided tape
Fountain pen and black ink

1 Choose a favorite floral image, perhaps from a vintage postcard, and photocopy it onto an A4 sheet of tracing paper positioning the floral design at one end of the paper so that it will appear on the front cover of the folder when folded in half. For the inner lining pages cut the Pergamenata paper to 8¼ x 11½in (21 x 29.7cm) using pencil, ruler, craft knife, and cutting board.

2 Fold the photocopied tracing papers in half to 8¼ x 5¾in (21 x 14.8cm). Repeat this with the semi-translucent paper using a bone folder as this paper is of a heavier weight. Glue the lining inside the tracing paper folder with spray adhesive by spraying ¼in (5mm) along the back fold of semi-translucent paper, masking off all other areas, then press to adhere against the spine. For the fastening, glue a glass button at the front using a spot of the multi-purpose adhesive. Cut a 48in (120cm) length of the gold thread for the fastening.

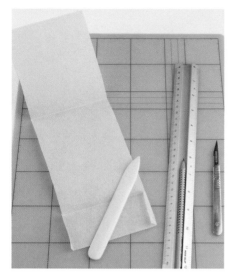

3 Using the template on page 141 cut out an envelope from the semi-translucent paper to a length of 13½in (33.5cm) using a cutting board and craft knife. With the wrong side of the paper facing you use the bone folder to crease the fold marks as indicated on the template.

HINT

Intriguing and collectable vintage postcards are an inspiration for the sheer variety of the illustrative styles and typography, stamps and postage marks, evocative messages, and charming handwriting. A small collection of French and English postcards dating from early 1900s to the 1950s and all featuring illustrations of roses show how unassuming simplicity often has the most charm. The images photocopy well on differing types of paper including tracing paper—just make sure the weight is compatible with the photocopying machine.

4 Cover the right sides of the two side flaps with the spray adhesive, first being careful to mask off the surrounding areas. Fold the bottom flap upward, positioning over the side flaps, to form the envelope. Cut a 4in (10cm) length of gold thread, fold it in two, and knot the ends together to form a loop. Attach it in the center of the top edge using a spot of multi-purpose glue. Glue a glass button to the 'pocket' of the envelope in a position to take the loop of thread when the top flap of the envelope is folded over.

5 Write your 'thank-you' message with fountain pen and black ink on a 3½ x 4⅜in (9 x 11cm) sheet of 'laid' paper. Insert this vertically into the pocket along with a decorative card and photo. Fasten the loop around the button, place into the folder, and fix with a piece of double-sided tape. Fold the thread in half and loop the folded end around the glass button, wrap the two ends around the folder and then several times around the button to fasten securely.

Templates

Use the following templates to make up the designs from the projects. For some you will need to enlarge the template by the percentage given. The tinted areas denote the outside of the projects.

——————————— cut line

– – – – – – – fold line

·························· pleat line

 glue area

Wedding invitation envelope page 14.
Enlarge by 300%

Floral invitation envelope page 24.
Enlarge by 200%

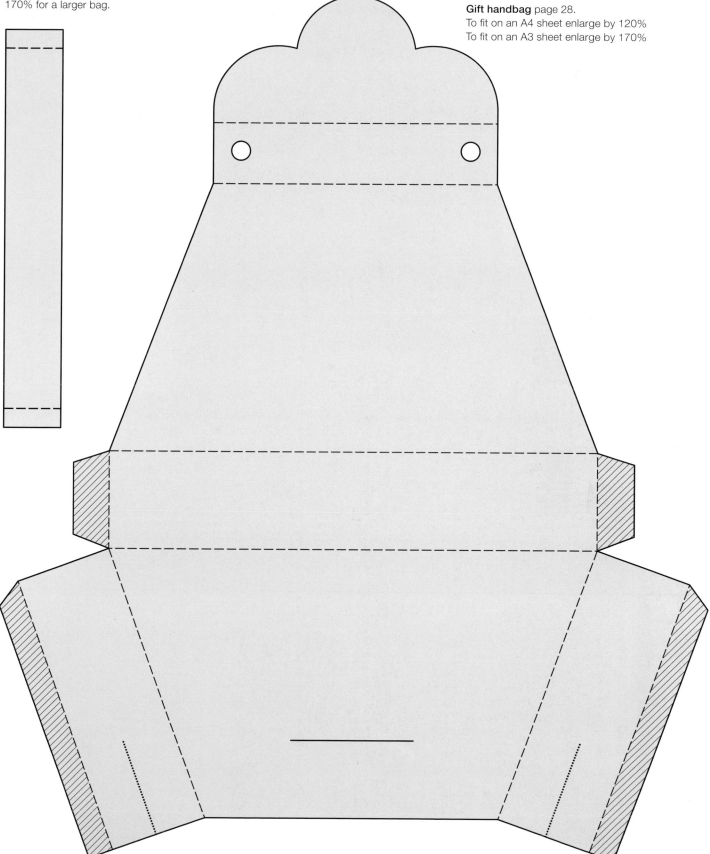

Gift handbag handle page 31.
Enlarge by 120% for a smaller bag,
170% for a larger bag.

Gift handbag page 28.
To fit on an A4 sheet enlarge by 120%
To fit on an A3 sheet enlarge by 170%

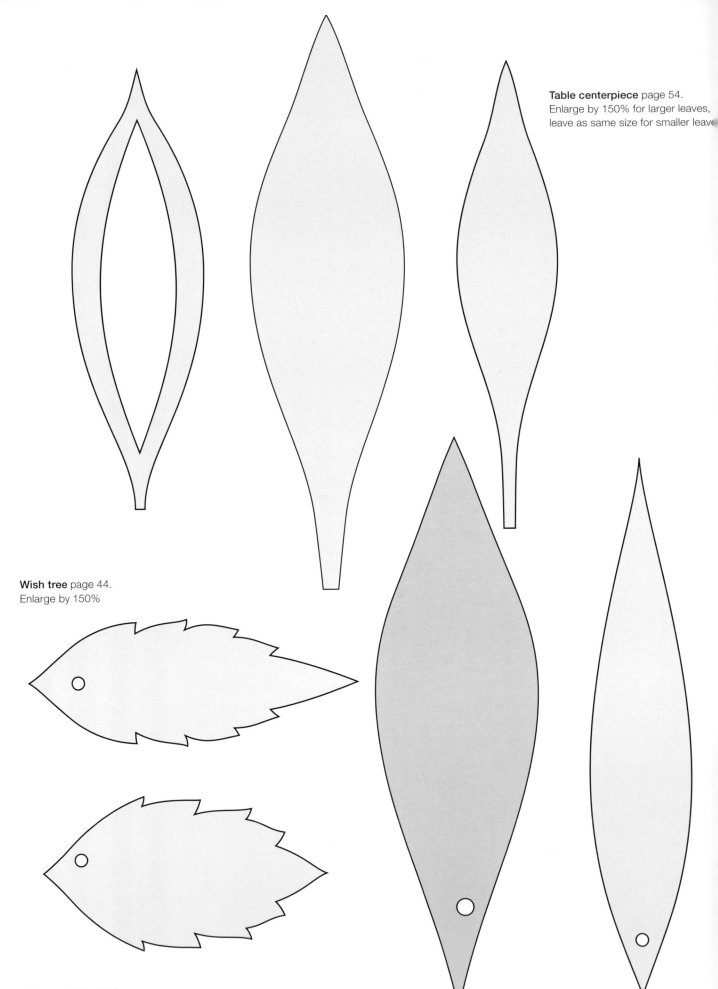

Table centerpiece page 54.
Enlarge by 150% for larger leaves,
leave as same size for smaller leave

Wish tree page 44.
Enlarge by 150%

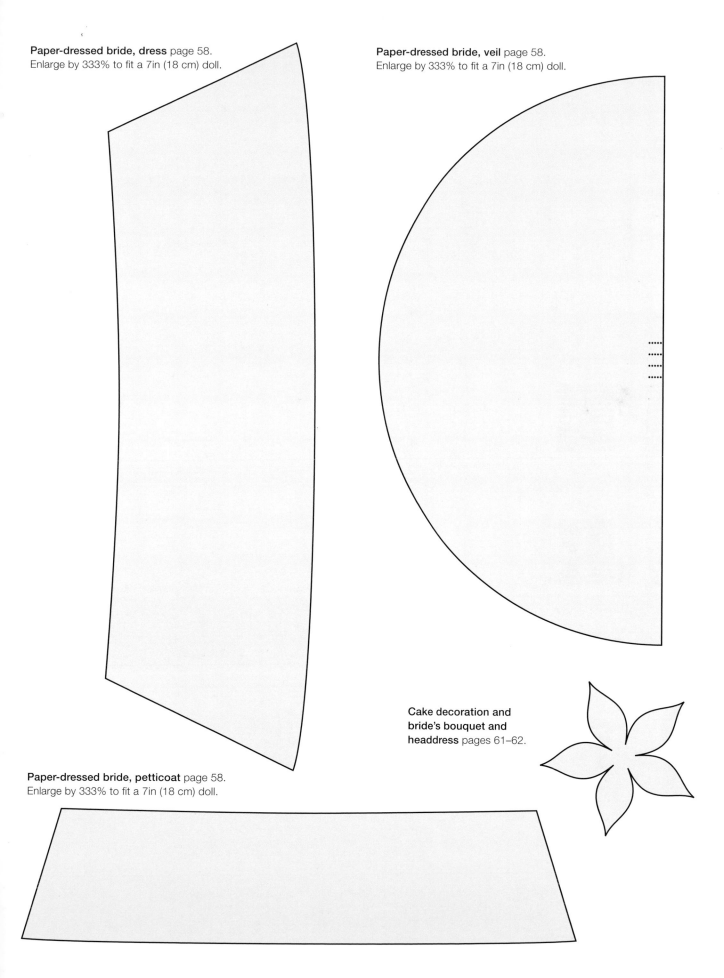

Paper-dressed bride, dress page 58.
Enlarge by 333% to fit a 7in (18 cm) doll.

Paper-dressed bride, veil page 58.
Enlarge by 333% to fit a 7in (18 cm) doll.

Cake decoration and
bride's bouquet and
headdress pages 61–62.

Paper-dressed bride, petticoat page 58.
Enlarge by 333% to fit a 7in (18 cm) doll.

Moiré box, base, and lid page 64.
Enlarge by:
115% for outer base
105% for inner base
115% for outer lid
100% for inner lid

Flower gift wrapping, petal page 70.
Enlarge by 143% for larger petals, leave as
same size for smaller petals.

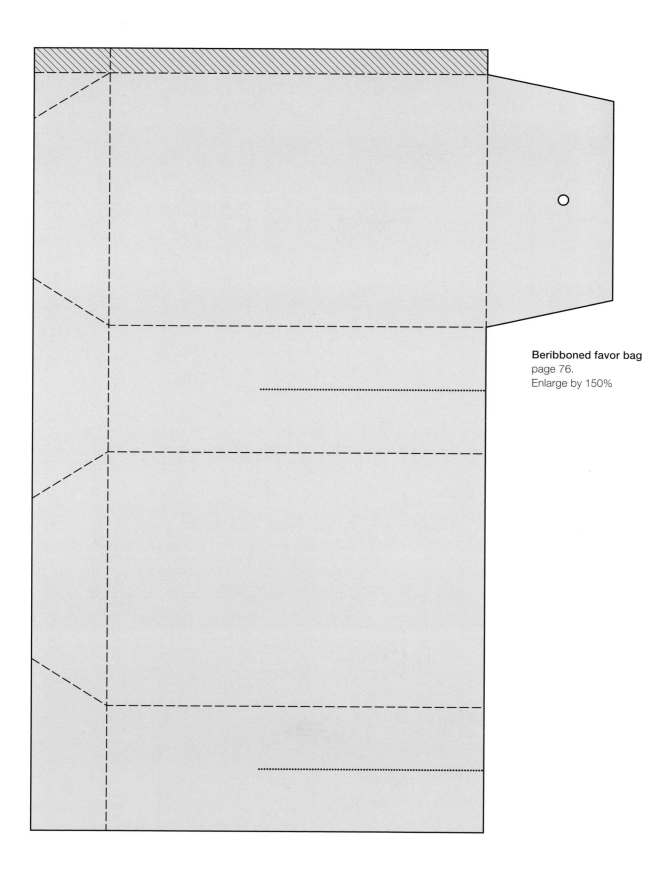

Beribboned favor bag
page 76.
Enlarge by 150%

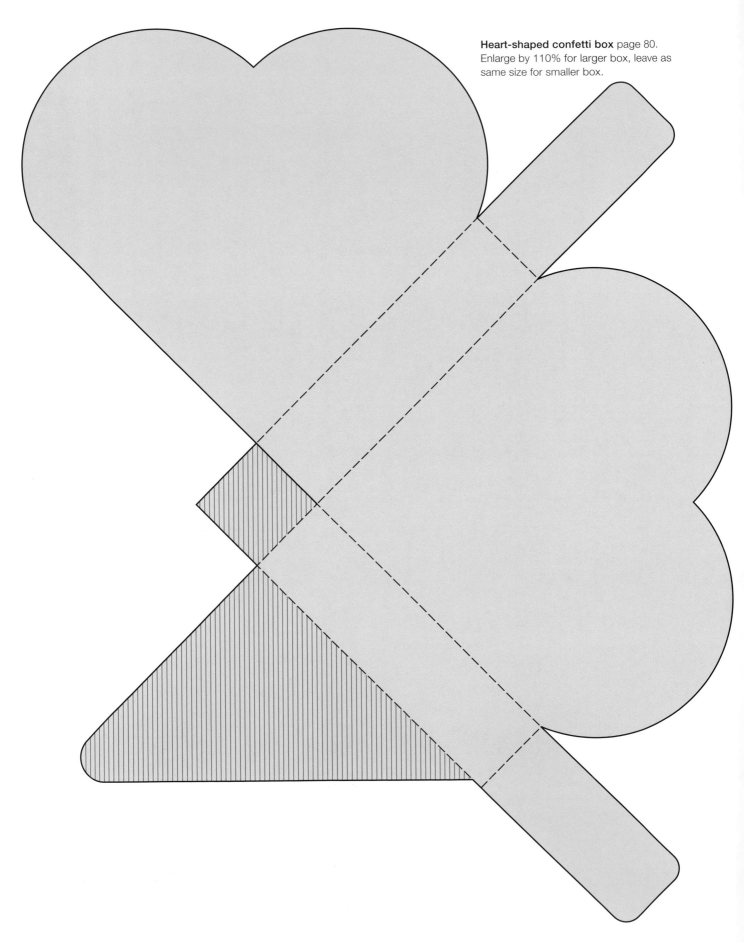

Heart-shaped confetti box page 80.
Enlarge by 110% for larger box, leave as same size for smaller box.

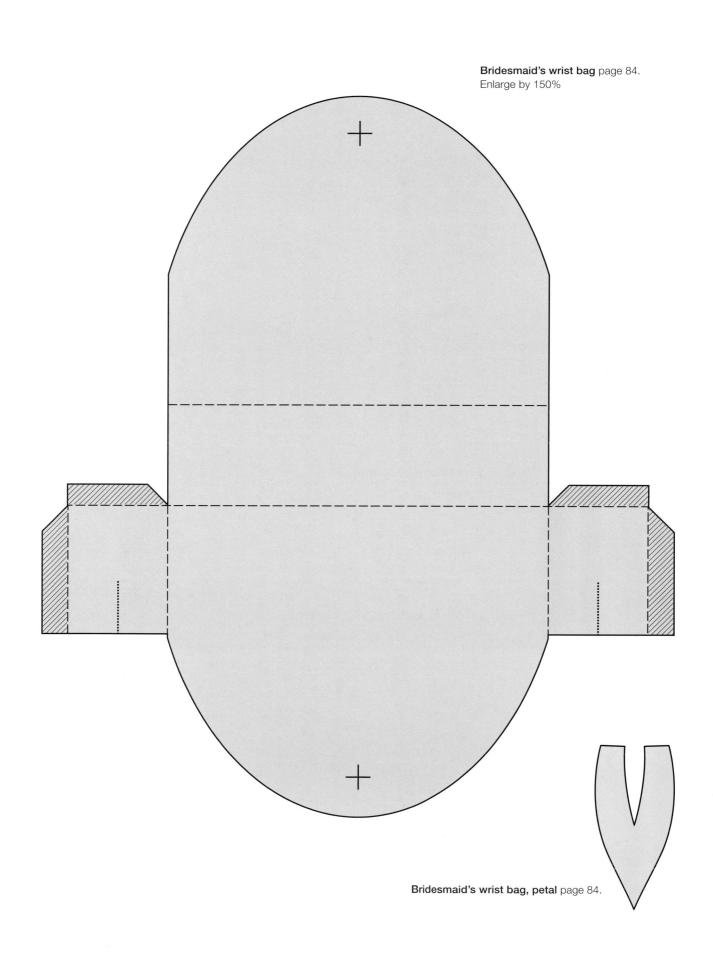

Bridesmaid's wrist bag page 84.
Enlarge by 150%

Bridesmaid's wrist bag, petal page 84.

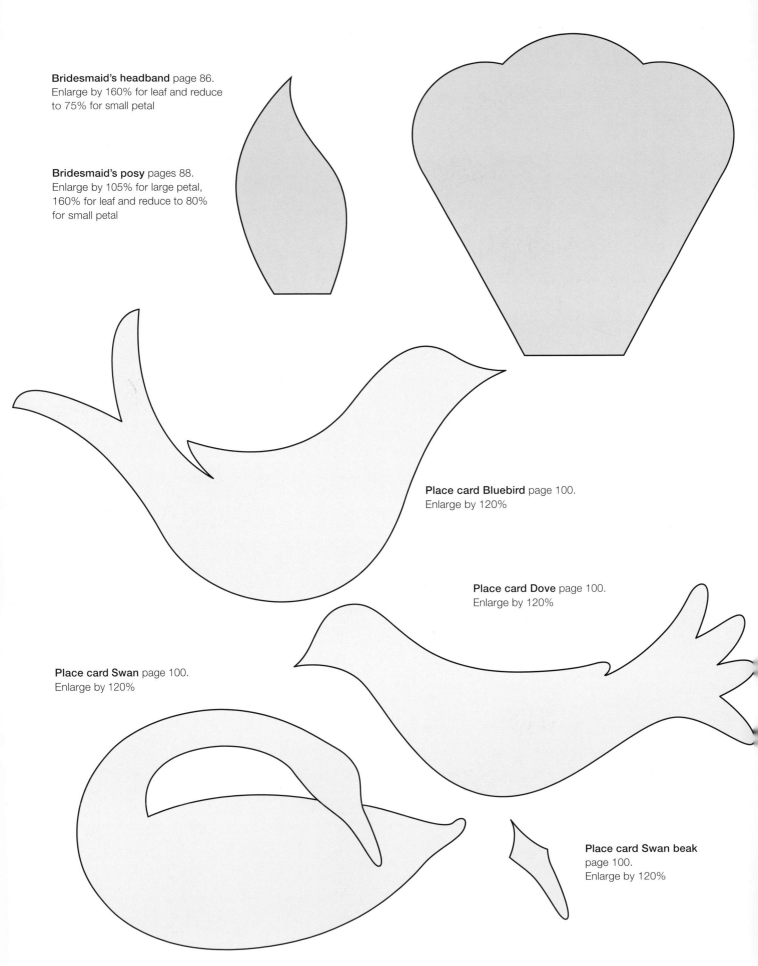

Bridesmaid's headband page 86.
Enlarge by 160% for leaf and reduce
to 75% for small petal

Bridesmaid's posy pages 88.
Enlarge by 105% for large petal,
160% for leaf and reduce to 80%
for small petal

Place card Bluebird page 100.
Enlarge by 120%

Place card Dove page 100.
Enlarge by 120%

Place card Swan page 100.
Enlarge by 120%

Place card Swan beak
page 100.
Enlarge by 120%

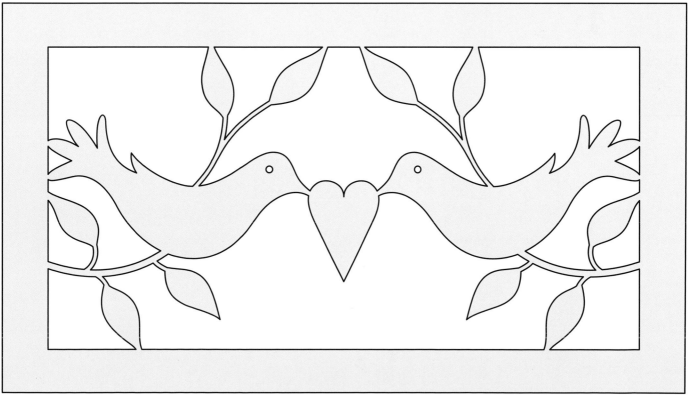

Children's invitation pages 92 and 95.
Enlarge by 125%

Table runner page 96.
Enlarge by 110%

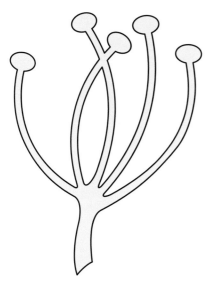

Beribboned cone page 102.
Enlarge by 110%

Table runner, continued page 96.
Enlarge by 110%

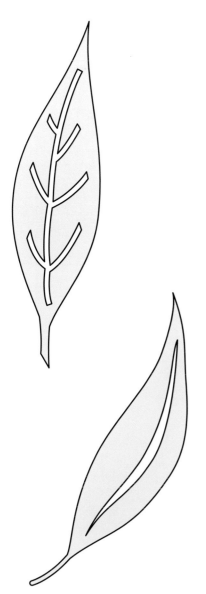

Favor carrier bag page 104.
Enlarge by 200%

Favor carrier bag, handle page 104.
Enlarge by 200%

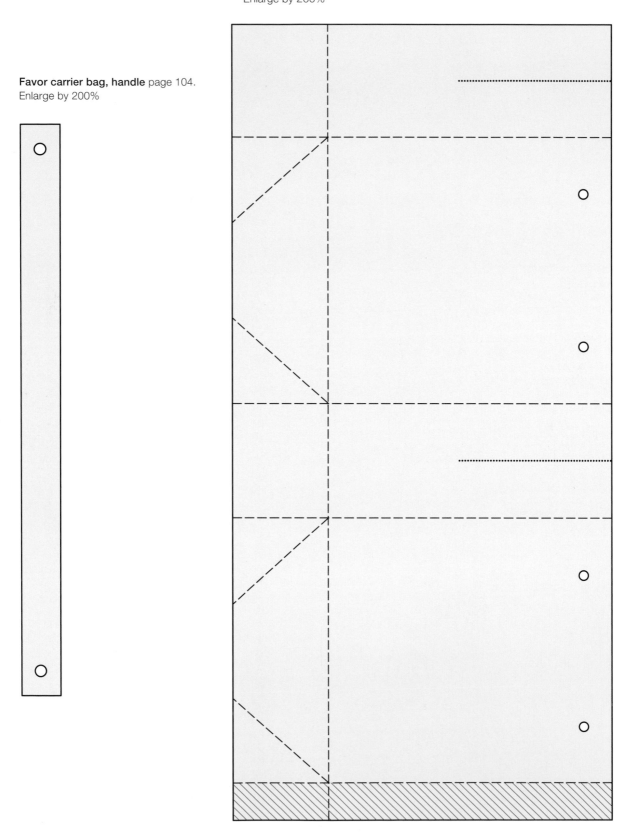

Thank you folder envelope page 127.
Enlarge by 140%

Hat box design page 118.
Enlarge as necessary to fit the hat
box of your choice.

Suppliers

US

Art Supplies Online, Minneapolis, MN
Stockists of decorative paper and art supplies
Tel: 1-800-967-7367
www.artsuppliesonline.com

Bella Rosa Paper Arts, Oshkosh, WI
Handmade and exotic papers
Tel: 1-920-233-5184
www.bellarosapaperarts.com

The Button Emporium, Portland, OR
Wide range of buttons, ribbons, and braid
Tel: 1-503-228-6372
www.buttonemporium.com

Camela Nitschke Ribbonry, Perrysburg, OH
Vintage and imported ribbons
Tel: 1-419-872-0073
www.ribbonry.com

Caspari Ltd., Seymour, CT
Suppliers of silver and gold moiré printed
paper tablecovers
Tel: 1-800-227-7274
www.casparionline.com

Crafts etc.
Stockists of decorative paper and art supplies
Tel: 1-800-888-0321
www.craftsetc.com

Craft Site Directory
Useful online resource
www.craftsdirectory.com

Darice, Strongsville, OH
Stockists of paper and art materials
Tel: 1-866-432-7423
www.darice.com

Hobby Lobby
Wide selection of paper and craft material
Stores nationwide
www.hobbylobby.com

Jo-ann Fabric & Craft
Craft suppliers with stores nationwide
Tel: 1-888-739-4120
www.joann.com

Kate's Paperie, New York, NY
Suppliers of moiré tissue paper, Japanese and
decorative papers, and craft supplies including
Cavallini stamps
Tel: 1-800-809-9880
www.katespaperie.com

Michaels
Comprehensive arts and crafts suppliers
Stores nationwide
www.michaels.com

Paper & Ink Arts, Woodsboro, MD
Supplies for book and paper artists
Tel: 1-301-845-9845
www.paperinkarts.com

Paper Source
Stores nationwide
www.paper-source.com

The Ribbonerie Inc., San Francisco, CA
Extensive collection of ribbons including
grosgrain, satin, and vintage
Tel: 1-415-626-6184
www.theribbonerie.com

UK

Alfie's Antique Market, London
Tel: 020 7723 6066
www.alfiesantiques.com

Antium Antiques at Hampstead Antique and
Craft Emporium, London
Jewelry from the 1940s–1950s
Tel: 07974 667801

Brissi, London
Silver-clad furniture and tableware
Tel: 0844 800 9912
www.brissi.co.uk

Button Lady, London
Antique buttons, buckles, and hatpins
Tel: 020 7435 5412
www.buttonladyhampstead.co.uk

Caspari Ltd., Essex
Suppliers of silver and gold moiré printed
paper tablecovers
Tel: 01799 513011
www.casparionline.com

Cass Art, London
Stocks a comprehensive range of art materials
Tel: 020 7354 2999
www.cassart.co.uk

The Cloth House, London
A range of unusual fabric including 'paper'
and 'polyethylene synthetic' fabrics
Tel: 020 7287 1555
www.clothhouse.com

The Dining Room Shop, London
Antique glass and tableware
Tel: 020 8878 1020
www.thediningroomshop.co.uk

Durham Dales Centre, Weardale,
Co. Durham
Stockists of moiré tissue
Tel: 01388 527650
www.durhamdalescentre.co.uk

East West Antiques & Books at
Alfie's Antique Market, London
Tel: 07708 863760

Fired Earth
High quality paint range
Stores nationwide
Tel: 0845 366 0400
www.firedearth.com

Hill Rise Interiors, Richmond, Surrey
A beautiful interiors boutique
Tel: 020 8940 1222
www.hillriseinteriors.co.uk

Liberty, London
Leading London department store including
haberdashery and wallpaper
Tel; 020 7734 1234
www.liberty.co.uk

Memories, London
Edwardian picture postcards and photographs
Tel: 020 8203 1500
www.memoriespostcards.co.uk

Paperchase
Specialists in imported and effect paper
Stores nationwide
www.paperchase.co.uk

Persiflage at Alfie's Antique Market, London
Vintage buttons, lace, and ribbons
Tel: 020 7724 7366
www.alfiesantiques.com

Geoffrey Robinson at
Alfie's Antique Market, London
Specialists in antique glassware
Tel: 07955 085723
www.alfiesantiques.com

VV Rouleaux, London
Ribbons, trims, and vintage bridal headdresses
Tel: 020 7730 3125
www.vvrouleaux.com

Sally Bourne Interiors, London
Homeware and Cavallini rubber stamps
Tel: 020 8340 3333
www.sallybourneinteriors.co.uk

Savoir Design, London
Bespoke wedding cakes by Eric Lanlard
Tel: 020 7978 5555
www.savoirdesign.com

Shepherds Bookbinders/Falkiners Fine
Papers, London
Fine papers including decorative Japanese
papers, Pergamenata and parchment,
patterned and watercolor papers
Tel: 020 7831 1151
www.falkiners.com

Index

Note: **Bold** page numbers refer to Templates